Copyright © 2021 by Maria A. Perez

All rights reserved.

No part of this book may be reproduced in any form or by any electronic or mechanical means, including information storage and retrieval systems, without written permission from the author, except for the use of brief quotations in a book review.

Published by: Maria A. Perez

ISBN: 978-1-7351133-4-0

Ebook ISBN: 978-1-7351133-5-7

Content Disclosure: Although not erotica, this book features romantic and sensual themes that may not be appropriate for audiences under 18.

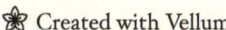 Created with Vellum

MONTOR'S SECRET STASH OF POEMS

A companion book to The Curse Of Sotkari Ta series

MARIA A. PEREZ

DEDICATION

The poems in this book are written from the point of view of Montor, a character in my romantic space opera series, The Curse of Sotkari Ta.

We learn that he is an unlikely poet with a secret stash of poems, most of them inspired by love.

And so, I dedicate this book to my love, Carlos.

CONTENTS

Books By This Author	xiii
Preface	xv
Bond	1
Chaos of Love	2
Whirlwind	3
Light	4
Dilemma	5
Journey	6
Dreams	7
Mocking Fate	8
Scar	9
Mirage	10
Daybreak	11
DNA	12
Teacher	13
Shots	14
Surprise	15
Debt	16
OK to Pray	17
Impulse	18
Witness	19
Murmurs	20
Curvy	21
Waiting	22
Imposter	23
Time	24
Trade	25
Stay	26
Shoreline	27

Incarcerated	28
Request	29
Patience	30
Ocean	31
Truth	32
Sweet Spots	33
Sexy Curves	34
Exploration	35
Aroma	36
Meditations	37
Erasure	38
Entertainment	39
Perfection	40
Caution	41
Sweet and Smooth	42
Lust	43
Contradiction	44
Overload	45
Temptation	46
Curls	47
Time	48
Lazy Morning	49
Cadence	50
Mystery	51
Rag	52
Darkness	53
Unannounced	54
Bankrupt	55
Loss	56
Decisions	57
Propel	58
Routes	59
Market Treats	60
Hollow Promises	61
Tortured	62

Advocate	63
Alone	64
Ache	65
Song	66
Scroll	67
Steps	68
Offing	69
Lesson	70
Kix	71
Dark and Light	72
Patrol	73
Abstain	74
Energy	75
Guide	76
Avalanche	77
Intertwined	78
Direction	79
Addiction	80
Consequences	81
Sweetness	82
Door	83
Courage	84
Blossom	85
Seasons	86
Rush	87
Huge	88
Facade	89
Questions	90
Trigger	91
Revelation	92
Sexy Telepathy	93
Readings	94
Wildflower	95
Unlocked	96
Gift	97

Surrender	98
Pressed	99
Otherworldly	100
So Much Love	101
Assurances	102
Flame Tree	103
Distraction	104
Memorable	105
Conundrum	106
Thief	107
Slip	108
Murderous Charade	109
From Tragedy to Hope	110
Always New	111
Games	112
Introductions	113
Exploration	114
Fool	115
Shooting Star	116
Candlelight	117
Embrace	118
Caress	119
Revenge	120
Memory	121
Mood	122
Signal	123
Tongue	124
Late	125
Release	126
Tease	127
Sure	128
Vacillations	129
Oasis	130
Rescue	131
Everything Has Changed	132

Charm	133
Secret Stash of Poems	134
A Note from the Author	135
Acknowledgments	137
About the Author	139

BOOKS BY THIS AUTHOR

The Curse of Sotkari Ta: Book One

Broken Bonds, The Curse of Sotkari Ta: Book Two

Rising From The Curse, The Curse of Sotkari Ta: Book Three

Song of the Caged Warrior, The Curse of Sotkari Ta: Prequel

Montor's Secret Stash of Poems (A companion book to The Curse of Sotkari Ta series)

PREFACE

I had not written poetry in a long time. When I was younger, it was a way to express the sadness I entombed in the depths of my soul. After meeting her, the words I strung together reflected feelings new to me. Females and their bodies had always been pleasant recreation. This was different.

These emotions—the passion. The admiration. The need to be close to her. At first, I did not want these things and never expected to experience such a loss of control. I felt it did not suit me and my lifestyle. Then, to my surprise, I fell in love. There was nothing more glorious than when we made love, nothing more depressing than when we were apart.

I had planned to keep these poems hidden from her. One day, we began to share pieces of ourselves—our pasts, our vulnerabilities—that we had not uncovered before. I found myself admitting I wrote poetry. Of course, she insisted on hearing a sample. Embarrassed and feeling foolish, I agonized over reading them aloud, but she loved them. She found them romantic and sweet. This led to more vigorous than usual lovemaking. She called them Montor's Secret Stash of Poems.

BOND

Hand in hand we go
Against all odds we struggle
A forever bond

CHAOS OF LOVE

My life is a mess
A cluttered chaos of love
You in the center

WHIRLWIND

Like a whirlwind
She blew in
Without warning
Life became
Exhilaration and Devastation

LIGHT

Golden jewelry
Amber eyes reflect the light
Guide to paradise

DILEMMA

Is it a mistake?
Love can be the enemy
Will my heart stay safe?
Should I unleash my passion
Or keep it locked up inside?

JOURNEY

Please show me the way
Across your hills and valleys
Till you shout my name

DREAMS

Close my eyes and dream
Of your lips, and taste, and tongue
Until our next kix[1]

---

1. "Kix" reflects Montor's pronunciation of the word "kiss," a word that does not exist in his language.

MOCKING FATE

I laugh at you, fate
Our paths should have never crossed
Yet we share one bed

SCAR

You left a scar on my heart
A keepsake of our time together

MIRAGE

The idyllic mirage vanished
The harsh desert reappeared
I was alone once again
You giggled and ran
Hiding under the covers
Catch me if you can

DAYBREAK

How marvelous
To open your eyes
One day
And say
I am in Love

DNA

You and Me
So different
Yet we share
Something
So basic
Our DNA

TEACHER

Close my eyes, stop thinking
Inhale her perfume and dream
Show me how to kix[1]

---

1. "Kix" reflects Montor's pronunciation of the word "kiss," a word that does not exist in his language.

SHOTS

A double shot, please
I need to forget her smile
And drown in my sorrow

SURPRISE

She surprises me
Her lust is as fierce as mine
How lucky am I

DEBT

Nothing can pacify
The anger
The rage
But I will make them pay

OK TO PRAY

It is OK to pray
Even if you do not believe
Love still finds a way

IMPULSE

What crazy impulse
Drives me to wake up each day
Thinking of your smile

WITNESS

Sweat glistens
Your skin
A witness
To the heat
Between
You and me

MURMURS

What do I hear murmuring?
My soul admitting
How much
We miss you

CURVY

It starts with your lips
The curvy road to desire
And ends with your hips

WAITING

Left with memories
Of her curves and aroma
I wait, patiently

IMPOSTER

An imposter
Pretending to be strong
Yet you bring me
To my knees

TIME

Time, irrelevant
When my pleasure is to taste
Every inch of you

TRADE

I offer a trade
My never-ending passion
Your eternal love

STAY

I fear nothing
Yet I cannot summon
The courage
To let you go

SHORELINE

She is the shoreline
I am the thrash of the waves
A hot summer's eve

INCARCERATED

Incarcerated
No locked doors or windows
Just sad without you

REQUEST

I gave it my best
Opened up my soul to you
Take care of the rest

PATIENCE

It should be simple
A matter of self-control
My patience fails me
Do I want to rebuke her
Or make sweet love all night long?

OCEAN

Dare I dip into
Her ocean of ecstasy
And drown forever

TRUTH

Being vulnerable
Not my thing
But somehow
She sees the
Truth in me

SWEET SPOTS

I envy the sea
It can boast having kix[1] *you*
In all those sweet spots

---

1. "Kix" reflects Montor's pronunciation of the word "kiss," a word that does not exist in his language.

SEXY CURVES

I entrust my brain
To never forget
The sexy curves
Of her hips

EXPLORATION

My hands explore
Aching to discover
The mysteries
Of her crests and valleys

AROMA

I kneel and inhale
The aroma of her skin
She leans into me

MEDITATIONS

Bury my sorrow
Forget the broken childhood
The young boy taken
Special powers lie within
I am no victim, I can mend

ERASURE

Is it possible
She erased her memory
And forgot my love?

ENTERTAINMENT

Entertain me
With a smile
A touch
And the sway
Of your hips

PERFECTION

Our time together
So brief, but pure perfection
Nothing quite the same

CAUTION

Ignore the heat
Best to be cautious
Must not give my heart away

SWEET AND SMOOTH

Her eyes remind me
Of the sweet taste of honey
And smooth brandy heat

LUST

When we Make Love
Nothing else Matters
Vigorous and Robust
A Lusty Connection

CONTRADICTION

An amazing feat
To love where there should be hate
All from just a touch

OVERLOAD

Her soft skin
Beautiful eyes
Luscious lips
Bombard my senses
A sensual overload

TEMPTATION

My hands, her bare skin
Smooth and supple temptation
Can I make her mine?

CURLS

Love the texture
Of her glossy hair
Soft curls
Splayed on my pillow

TIME

I will take my time
To get to know your body
Each minute a dream

LAZY MORNING

A lazy morning
No rush to get out of bed
When our bodies touch

CADENCE

A perfect cadence
In my dream, our bodies joined
Our heat, yes, intense

MYSTERY

Countless steps
Pacing back and forth
A mystery
A heartache
Where is she?

RAG

Ripped, tattered, and torn
A rag that has been through too much
No way to soak up
The torrential tears I hide
So I cry behind my smile

DARKNESS

Dark future, black hole
Where my molecules explode
Yes, I still miss her

UNANNOUNCED

A smile, a touch
Suddenly
She is becoming
The rest of my life

BANKRUPT

My soul is bankrupt
Yet each day I pay the price
For daring to hope

LOSS

My plan went askew.
I did not think I would lose her.
Who knew?

DECISIONS

Trying to decide
Her eyes, honey or brandy?
Highlight of my day

PROPEL

Propel me into a reality
Where her amber eyes
Greet me every morning

ROUTES

Traveling your curves
The various routes excite me
A glorious trip

MARKET TREATS

Her body is like a market
With so many treats to try out

HOLLOW PROMISES

I will look for you
And we will be together
When the time is right
Now just a hollow promise
Death has made a fool of me

TORTURED

My tortured instinct
Arrogant and unpleasant
Conceals my true soul

ADVOCATE

I need an advocate
Tell her I am here
Waiting
Dead
Until she returns

ALONE

I wake up alone
She is far away by now
My soul left with her

ACHE

When I touch her hand
The sensual energy
Irresistible
Confuses and confounds me
I ache to discover more

SONG

Her voice is a song
My heart strives to remember
The beat and cadence
The melody, the texture
How my name rolled off her tongue

SCROLL

I unravel and spread her out
A treasured scroll that requires careful study
Softly licking my fingers
In trembling anticipation
Careful to trace
The subtle curvature of each letter
Every word whispered upon my lips
A silent prayer in reverence of her form
Laid out before me

STEPS

My soul said, endure
These are only the first steps
The journey is long
Our love is a destiny
I dare not question such things

OFFING

The Offing
Sea meets Sky
A Breathtaking and Dangerous
Union
You and I

LESSON

Each night a lesson
As we become one, I learn
How to make her shout

KIX

Her lips meet my lips
Slips her tongue in to meet mine
Teach me how to kix[1]

---

1. "Kix" reflects Montor's pronunciation of the word "kiss," a word that does not exist in his language.

DARK AND LIGHT

A child of the dark
Became an angry adult
She brought me to light

PATROL

My mind goes on patrol
To keep my heart in check
Too late

ABSTAIN

Abstain
From thinking
About
Her smile?
Easier
To stop
My heart
From beating

ENERGY

Bouncing light
Candles flicker
Our hands touch
Energy transfers
Our eyes meet
The start
Of forever

GUIDE

The light of her eyes
Guides me through my darkest day
Helps me see the way

AVALANCHE

It took me by surprise
This avalanche of emotion
My love for you

INTERTWINED

Our fates intertwined
Nothing can pull us apart
A promise of love

DIRECTION

My heart always
Steers me
In the right direction
To where she is

ADDICTION

She can be so bad
Her touch is an addiction
But it feels so good

CONSEQUENCES

Feel rather than think
Forget the consequences
What she does to me

SWEETNESS

Her lustrous eyes
The color of honey
Is why I call her
Sweetness

DOOR

How did she open
With just a smile and a touch
The door to my soul

COURAGE

Admirable
Resistant to evil
Her soft strength
Taught me
The meaning
Of courage

BLOSSOM

Like a blossom
Both delicate and bold
Her love opens up to me

SEASONS

Days turn into nights
Rainy season floods the land
Cool weather follows
Time goes on as we revolve
Only my love stays steady

RUSH

First a heated rush
Of course, once is not enough
Now we take our time

HUGE

Her eyes opened wide
Ready for love, I disrobed
She shouts, you are huge!

FACADE

My cocky attitude
Just a pretense
The appearance
Of indifference
Just a facade

QUESTIONS

How did we get here?
We traveled this road so quickly
What should we do now?

TRIGGER

Triggered by a touch
The energy between us
Confirmed by a kix[1]

---

1. "Kix" reflects Montor's pronunciation of the word "kiss," a word that does not exist in his language.

REVELATION

How did she do it?
Changed my outlook and revealed
Best version of me

SEXY TELEPATHY

I can read her mind
And see what is her pleasure
A sexy surprise

READINGS

She asked that I read
The poems I wrote for her
Not an easy task

WILDFLOWER

Unsophisticated Charm
Disheveled and Random
Bold and Beautiful
Strong and Resistant
My wildflower
She takes my breath away

UNLOCKED

She made me reveal
Long kept secrets and feelings
My passion unlocked

GIFT

I walked in darkness
You are the light
Born of my seed
The same but different
A miracle of love
My son, my pride
Her gift to me

SURRENDER

All my life I was loyal to no one
Now her supple body is the land I fight for
Her billowing hair is my flag
Her amber eyes form my crest
Her gentle laughter sings my battle hymn
Victory is her cheek against my chest
I have won and lost this war
She made me both her prisoner and patriot

PRESSED

Hands pressed together
Live this moment forever
Our bodies are one

OTHERWORLDLY

No one looks like her
She came from another world
Made my dreams come true

SO MUCH LOVE

When it comes to her
There is never enough time
To share so much love

ASSURANCES

Can you assure me
To be the first thing I see
Each and every day

FLAME TREE

Flame tree, red flowers
Your beauty has no rival
One would never guess
How far your strong roots extend
Like my love, never-ending

DISTRACTION

All I think of every day
Is how she and I can play
She licks her lips
And sways her hips
Lust will lead her my way

MEMORABLE

A foreign surprise
Is not what I expected
Memorable ride

CONUNDRUM

How can I heal
Her tempestuous soul
When I am
The source of the storm

THIEF

I did not expect
She would be so efficient
Thief who stole my heart

SLIP

My hands find their way
The ball gown slips to the floor
Nothing underneath

MURDEROUS CHARADE

This charade must end
Our love should not be hidden
Kills me every day

FROM TRAGEDY TO HOPE

Merciless memory
You fickle trickster
Forget the tragedy
So I can hope again

ALWAYS NEW

Instead of
Becoming routine
Each time we touch
My passion for her
Multiplies

GAMES

Fate, what game is this?
Could she be my destiny?
Please play by the rules

INTRODUCTIONS

Raised without loved ones
Bitterness and suffering
Were the daily bread
Now it dares to care again
I present to you my heart

EXPLORATION

My finger explores
Secret spots that make her shout
Don't stop she implores

FOOL

I thought I was strong
Love made a fool out of me
I can live with that

SHOOTING STAR

*You illuminated
My world
Like a flash of light
A shooting star
That enchanted my night
Then vanished
Without warning*

CANDLELIGHT

It did not matter
Ambiance and candlelight
Soft music and wine
The truth still hung in the air
I could never call her mine

EMBRACE

Her hands on my chest
Our bodies pressed together
In a hot embrace

CARESS

Her loving caress
Pulls me away
From an empty life
Towards my destiny

REVENGE

No space in my heart
To forgive those who harmed her
I will seek revenge
A jealous rage consumes me
They will know my agony

MEMORY

As night turns to day
The memory of her touch
Is never-ending

MOOD

We are like-minded
A touch is all we need
To get us in the mood

SIGNAL

When she is present
My world is a different place
The air is fragrant
Her perfume is a signal
That my happiness is near

TONGUE

I love how my name
Rolls off the tip of her tongue
When we become one

LATE

Did we meet too late?
Perhaps in some other place
We are just in time

RELEASE

Lie down
Relax
Let me help you
Relinquish control
Lure out that
Release

TEASE

I start with her toes
Her giggles motivate me
To work my way up

SURE

As sure as daybreak
Refreshing like morning dew
Is my love for her

VACILLATIONS

I vacillated
Between two worlds until love
Made me take a stand

OASIS

Thirsty and barren
A soul parched by suffering
Dried of emotion
Her love a lush oasis
Where I restored my passion

RESCUE

She rescued my soul
From a dark place
Where anger held me captive

EVERYTHING HAS CHANGED

Hands touch
Pulses accelerate
I pretend not to notice
That everything has changed

CHARM

How did she charm me?
Was it the bright amber eyes
Or her quiet strength?

SECRET STASH OF POEMS

Kept hidden
Until now
For her eyes only
My secret stash of poems

A NOTE FROM THE AUTHOR

Thank you for reading *Montor's Secret Stash of Poems*. Please consider taking a moment to write a review on Amazon, BookBub, and Goodreads. This means a lot to self-published authors such as me.

If you enjoyed Montor's poetry, maybe you might like to know more about him. He is a main character in the romantic space opera series, The Curse of Sotkari Ta. You can find the links to the completed trilogy, as well as all my social media links here:

https://direct.me/mariaaperezauthor

I would love to connect with you!

ACKNOWLEDGMENTS

I enjoy participating in many of the writing prompts hosted on Twitter by members of the writing community and feel so lucky to be a part of that group. In addition to the support I receive there, I now need to thank them for motivating me to try my hand at writing poetry. Once I decided that one of the characters in my romantic space opera series would be a secret poet, I found myself responding to the prompts by writing poems in his voice.

I am especially thankful for the following hosts who provided the prompts that inspired most of the poems contained in this book:

Evita Grazia, host of #HaikuLust (@HaikuLust)
Scott Christopher Beebe, host of #Poetryin13
Eve Castle, host of #TankaThursday
@baffled, host of #haikuchallenge
@Write2Fite, host of #BraveWrite

I am grateful to Migs (@OminousHallways) for collaborating with me on the poem titled "Surrender" and for his friendship and advice.

Big thanks to the talented Sam Steel (@SamJournals)

for allowing me to include his poem "Scroll" in this book. I enjoy our collaborations on #draftfolderfriday.

Thank you to my husband, sons, family, and friends who support me on this writing journey. Last, but not least, I thank my readers, current and future. I hope you enjoy my writing for many years to come.

ABOUT THE AUTHOR

Maria A. Perez was born in Yonkers, NY, and grew up in New York City. She also lived in Puerto Rico and now resides in Boca Raton, Florida. She holds a Bachelor's in Business and has spent a successful career in Corporate America working in Accounting and Finance. Early retirement has allowed Maria to focus on her dream of writing and becoming a published author. She is married with two young adult sons and a labradoodle daughter. Maria enjoys reading all genres, although she's partial to dystopian, space opera and romance series such as The Hunger Games, The Expanse and Outlander. A diehard "Trekkie" and Star Wars fan, she is fascinated with the possibility of what is out there in unexplored space and the potential of the human race.

Follow Maria at:
  Facebook.com/MariaAPerez.Author
  Twitter.com/MariaAPerez1
  Instagram.com/mariaaperezauthor

www.ingramcontent.com/pod-product-compliance
Lightning Source LLC
Chambersburg PA
CBHW060359080526
44583CB00012B/387